D0857546

Fly

BUG BOOKS

Karen Hartley, Chris Macro, and Philip Taylor

Heinemann Library
Chicago, IL

6/12/2008

WHITING PUBLIC LIBRARY
WHITING, IN 46394

© 2003, 2008 Heinemann Library
a division of Reed Elsevier Inc.
Chicago, Illinois

Customer Service 888-454-2279
Visit our website at www.heinemannlibrary.com

All rights reserved. No part of this publication may be reproduced or transmitted in any form or by any means, electronic or mechanical, including photocopying, recording, taping, or any information storage and retrieval system, without permission in writing from the publisher.

Design: Kimberly R. Miracle and Cavedweller Studio
Illustration: Alan Fraser at Pennant Illustration

Originated by Dot Gradations Ltd
Printed and bound in China by South China Printing Company

12 11 10 09 08
10 9 8 7 6 5 4 3 2 1

New edition ISBNs: 978 1 4329 1233 8 (hardcover)
                     978 1 4329 1244 4 (paperback)

The Library of Congress has cataloged the first edition as follows:
   Hartley, Karen, 1949-
    Fly / Karen Hartley, Chris Macro, Phillip Taylor
        p. cm. -- (Bug books)
    Summary: Describes the physical characteristics, habits, and natural
    environment of the fly.
    Includes bibliographical references (p.   ).
     ISBN 978-1-4329-1233-8 (hardcover) -- ISBN 978-1-4329-1244-4 (pbk.)
    1. Juvenile literature. [1. Fly.] I. Title:
    II. Title. III. Series.
     QL533.2.H36 2000
     595.77--dc21
                                    99-05741

Acknowledgments
The publishers would like to thank the following for permission to reproduce photographs:
© Ardea London pp. 7 (J. L. Mason), 9 (Alan Weaving), 10 (P. Morris), 16 (Pascal Goetgheluck), 28 (Pascal Goetgheluck); © Bruce Coleman pp. 18 (Jane Burton), 20 (Felix Labhardt); © FLPA pp. 4 (B. Borell), 24; © Heather Angel p. 17; © Nature Photographers Ltd (Nicholas Phelps Brown) p. 23; © NHPA pp. 11, 12 (Stephen Dalton), 13 (Stephen Dalton), 14 (Stephen Dalton), 26 (Stephen Dalton); © Oxford Scientific Films pp. 5 (K .G. Vock), 8 (G. I. Bernard), 21 (Bob Fredrick), 22 (Andrew Plumptre), 25 (Avril Rampage), 27 (Stephen Dalton), 29 (London Scientific Films); © Photolibrary pp. 6 (Rafi Ben-Shahar), 15 (Richard Packwood), 19 (Elliot Neep).

Cover photograph of a greenbottle fly reproduced with permission of Science Photo Library (John Devries).

Every effort has been made to contact copyright holders of any material reproduced in this book. Any omissions will be rectified in subsequent printings if notice is given to the publisher.

Contents

Some words are shown in bold, **like this**. You can find out what they mean by looking in the glossary.

What Are Flies?

housefly

Flies are **insects**. There are many different types of fly. The flies we see most are houseflies and bluebottles.

4

eye

wing

antenna

leg

Flies have six legs and two wings.
Their eyes are very big. They have two
antennae that they use for smelling.

5

What Do Flies Look Like?

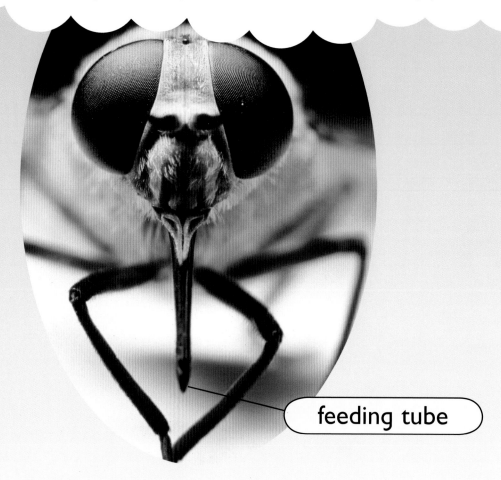

feeding tube

A fly does not have a mouth or teeth. It eats through a long tube at the front of its head. Flies have little holes in their bodies for breathing.

Flies can be lots of different colors. Bluebottle and greenbottle flies are shiny. This hover fly has bright yellow stripes.

How Big Are Flies?

Some flies are very small. The midge in this photo is not much bigger than the period at the end of this line.

Houseflies and bluebottles are fat and hairy. Crane flies are long and thin. This fly is called a robber fly. It can be as long as a man's finger!

How Are Flies Born?

egg

Houseflies and bluebottles lay hundreds of eggs. They lay them in rotting vegetables or in bad meat. Sometimes flies lay eggs in our food.

maggot

egg

After about two days the eggs **hatch**
into **larvae**. The larvae of bluebottles
and houseflies are called maggots.
The maggots wriggle around and look
for food.

How Do Flies Grow?

pupa

The maggots grow quickly and get too big for their skins. The old skin falls off and they grow a new one. This is called **molting**. After about ten days, the maggot turns into a hard case called a **pupa**.

Inside the pupa, the maggot changes into a fly. After about six days, the **adult** housefly crawls out of the hard pupa case.

pupa case

adult fly

How Do Flies Move?

Flies move very quickly through the air. Their wings make a buzzing sound as they fly.

14

Some very small flies move around in a big group. This is called **swarming**. A swarm can look like a cloud.

What Do Flies Eat?

Male bluebottles and houseflies suck up **nectar** from flowers. The **females** sometimes come into our kitchens and nibble our food.

Flies squirt juice onto their food. This makes the food get soft. The fly then sucks the food through its feeding tube. Some tiny flies suck blood from animals.

17

WHITING PUBLIC LIBRARY
WHITING, IN 46394

Which Animals Eat Flies?

spider

insect

web

Spiders like to eat flies. They catch flies
and other insects in their sticky webs.
Birds and frogs also eat flies.

18

Many animals eat the **larvae** of flies. Fish eat larvae that live near rivers and lakes. Many birds like to eat maggots.

Where Do Flies Live?

Flies live in most parts of the world.
Some flies live in shady places near water.
Others live near plants, fruit, and flowers.
These flies live on animal **droppings**.

Many **adult** flies live near rotting food and rubbish. The **larvae** can live underground or under the **bark** of trees.

How Long Do Flies Live?

pupa

adult fly

The housefly lives for about 21 days after it comes out of its **pupa** case. Most flies die when the weather gets cold, but some flies sleep through the winter.

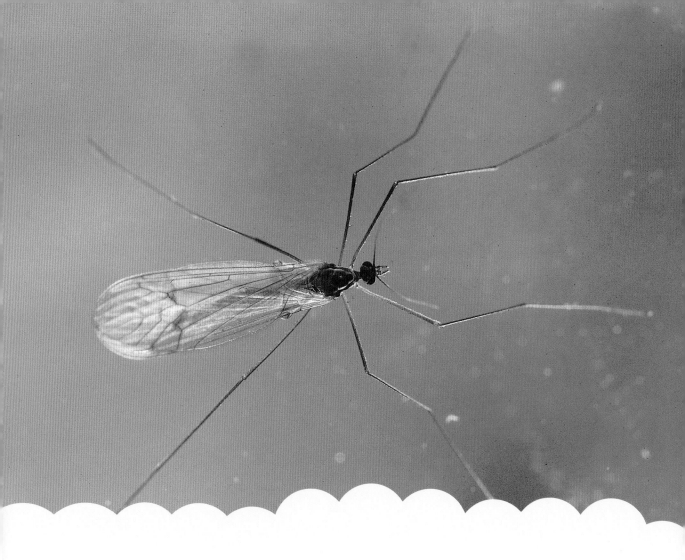

Some **adult** midges live only for one day. This is just long enough for the **female** to **mate** and lay her eggs.

What Do Flies Do?

Houseflies and bluebottles spend most of their time looking for food. The **females** often come into our houses.

24

Many flies are **pests**. They pick up **germs** from dirty places. The flies bring dirt and germs into our houses and onto our food.

How Are Flies Special?

Flies have sticky pads on their feet. The pads help them walk up windows. They can even walk upside down.

26

Flies have very special eyes. They are made of thousands of small parts. Each part sends a different picture to the fly's brain.

eye

Thinking About Flies

Here is a picture of a fly on some food. What will the fly do to the food so it can suck it up easily?

28

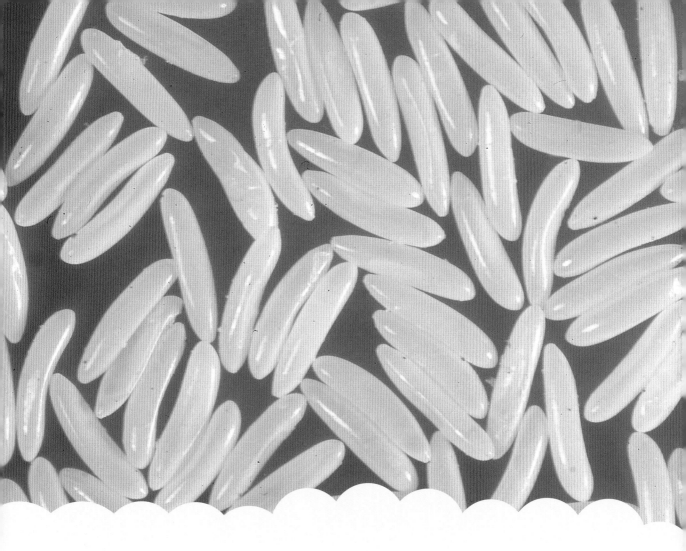

These housefly's eggs have just been laid. How long will it be before they **hatch** into **larvae?**

Bug Map

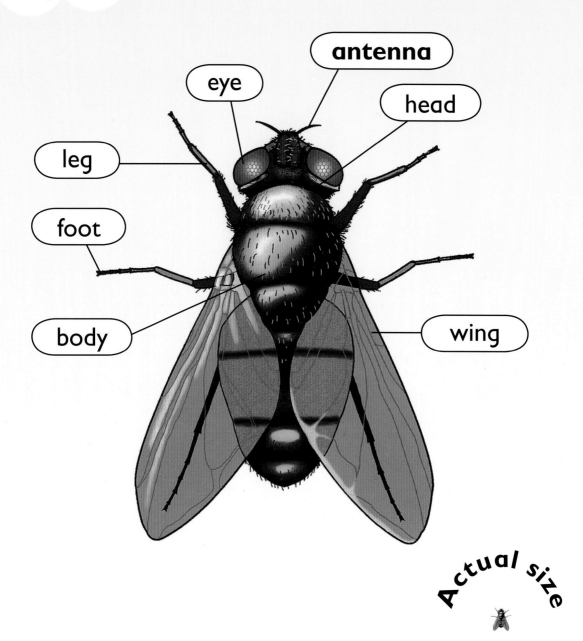

antenna

eye

head

leg

foot

body

wing

Actual size

30

Glossary

adult grown-up

antenna (more than one = antennae) thin tube that sticks out from the head of an insect. Antennae can be used to smell, feel, hear, or sense direction.

bark hard skin around a tree

droppings body waste from an animal

female animal that can lay eggs or give birth to young

germ tiny living thing that can get inside your body and make you ill

hatch to break out of an egg

insect small animal with six legs and a body with three parts

larva (more than one = larvae) baby insect that hatches from an egg. It does not look like the adult insect.

male animal that can mate with a female to produce young

mate when a male and female come together to make babies

molting time in an insect's life when it gets too big for its skin. The old skin drops off and a new skin is underneath.

nectar the sweet juice found inside flowers

pest an animal that causes damage or hurts other animals

pupa (more than one = pupae) larva with a hard case around its body before it turns into an adult

swarming when lots of insects fly very close to each other

Index

antennae 5, 30

bluebottles 4, 7, 9, 10, 11, 16, 24

color 7

eating 6, 16, 17, 18, 19, 28
eggs 10, 11, 23, 29
enemies 18, 19
eyes 5, 27, 30

germs 25
growing 12

hatching 11, 29
housefly 4, 9, 10, 11, 13, 16, 22, 24, 29

larvae 11, 19, 21, 29
legs 5, 30
lifespan 22, 23

maggots 11, 12, 13, 19
midge 8, 23
molting 12
movement 11, 14, 15, 26

pests 25
pupa 12, 13, 22

size 8, 9, 30
swarming 15

wings 5, 14, 30

More Books to Read

Harris, Nicholas. *First Library of Knowledge: World of Bugs.* Farmington Hills, MI: Blackbirch Press, 2006.

Phillips, Dee. *My First Book of Bugs and Spiders.* Tunbridge Wells, UK: Ticktock Media, 2005.

Ross, Stewart and Jim Pipe. *Minibeasts: Going on a Bug Hunt.* London: Franklin Watts, 2006.

WHITING PUBLIC LIBRARY
WHITING, IN 46394